# THE PERFORMANCE MANAGEMENT POCKETBOOK

## 2nd Edition

## By Pam Jones

*Drawings by Phil Hailstone*

"In an ever-demanding and competitive world, OK and average simp
performance matters. If you want to get the best out of your people,
packed with advice and ideas on how to do that."
**Lydia Hatley, Leadership Change Manager, Argos**

"Very useful – a practical and comprehensive guide for all leaders who truly
value their team."
**Claire Dobbs, Managing Director, Havas Life London.**

*Published by:*
**Management Pocketbooks Ltd**
Laurel House, Station Approach, Alresford, Hants SO24 9JH, U.K.
Tel: +44 (0)1962 735573   Fax: +44 (0)1962 733637
E-mail: sales@pocketbook.co.uk
Website: www.pocketbook.co.uk

© Pam Jones 1999, 2013

First edition 1999      ISBN 978 1 870471 65 7
This edition 2013       ISBN 978 1 906610 53 1   Reprinted 2015
E-book                  ISBN 978 1 908284 29 7

British Library Cataloguing-in-Publication Data – A catalogue record for this book is available from the British Library.

Design, typesetting and graphics by **efex Ltd.**    Printed in U.K.

# CONTENTS

## WHO SHOULD READ THIS BOOK

This book is for managers who care about their people and want to succeed through them and with them. It provides a clear understanding of performance management and the role of engagement. You will also find plenty of tips and techniques to enhance your performance in the following areas:

- Leading others to achieve results
- Understanding the impact of your own style
- Engaging and motivating others
- Creating high-performance teams
- Setting clear objectives
- Managing performance difficulties
- Coaching and delegating effectively

You may want to read the whole book or just focus on the area of most use to you at the moment.

# WHAT IS PERFORMANCE MANAGEMENT?

# THE BIGGER PICTURE

What is your definition of performance management?

Most people associate it with concepts such as:

- Appraisal
- Performance-related pay
- Targets and objectives
- Motivation and discipline

Yet, performance management is much more than this.

# A DEFINITION

Performance management is about **getting results.** It is concerned with getting the best from people and helping them to achieve their potential.

It is an approach to achieving a shared vision of the purpose and aims of the organisation. It is concerned with helping individuals and teams achieve their potential and recognise their role in contributing to the goals of the organisation.

**Manager**

**Organisation**

**Team**

**Individual**

# THE ROLE OF ENGAGEMENT

Employee engagement has an important role to play in performance management. It is the emotional commitment the employee has to the organisation and its goals. It is also about creating an environment where employees are motivated to want to connect with their work and really care about doing a good job. Without engagement, getting the best from people is an uphill struggle. *(Chartered Institute of Personnel and Development 2009)*

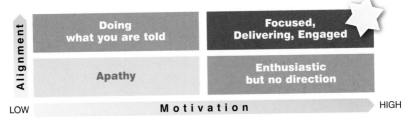

Motivation together with alignment leads to engagement.

# WHAT IS PERFORMANCE MANAGEMENT?

## ENGAGEMENT – CASE STUDY

**Situation:** Tom is a promising employee, who works for a retail organisation as a junior manager. His boss gives him a list of tasks each day and monitors his work. Tom is always informed when something isn't right.

Tom does his job but feels bored and uninvolved. No one asks his opinion and he has no idea about how to develop in his role. As a result, he works to a good enough standard but always looks forward to the end of the day.

**Question:** How engaged is Tom? What are the consequences of his behaviour both for him and for the organisation?

**Analysis:** Engagement is about building motivation and an emotional commitment to the organisation. The fact that Tom is not being involved, coached, praised or developed is having a negative impact on his performance. He is just doing his job, but could do a lot more. The likelihood is that Tom will leave. The organisation will have missed getting the most out of him and will incur all the expense and disruption of recruiting and training a new employee.

# ENGAGEMENT – CASE STUDY

**Situation:** Sunita works for a different organisation as a junior manager. Her boss involves her in team meetings and provides plenty of on-the-job coaching. Sunita receives regular feedback and is praised when she shows initiative. She is always trying to improve her performance and is happy to go the extra mile to help her colleagues and customers.

**Question:** What is different about Sunita's situation? What are the consequences for her and for the organisation?

**Analysis:** Sunita is very motivated. She feels valued and wants to do her best for the organisation. The organisation benefits from her energy and enthusiasm and this will impact on the overall results of the team.

# ENGAGEMENT – THE PROOF

There is plenty of proof that engaged employees deliver improved bottom line results, are more creative, stay with their organisations, have less time off work and deliver higher levels of customer satisfaction.

- Engaged employees generate 43% more revenue (Hay Group)

- Engaged employees: 2.7 sick days per year compared to 6.2 days from disengaged employees (Gallup)

- Engaged employees are 87% less likely to leave (Corporate Leadership Council)

- 67% of engaged advocate their organisations; only 3% of the disengaged do (Gallup)

- 59% of engaged employees say 'work brings out their most creative ideas' – only 3% of disengaged agree (Gallup)

## BUILDING ENGAGEMENT

The twelve questions below are used in many engagement surveys. They were developed by the Gallup organisation and their research shows that high scores for the questions correlate with improved bottom line performance. You can fill this questionnaire in for yourself or give it to your team to measure their level of engagement.*

Score

1. Do I know what is expected of me at work? ☐

2. Do I have the materials and equipment I need to do my work right? ☐

3. At work, do I have the opportunity to do what I do best every day? ☐

4. In the last seven days, have I received recognition or praise for doing good work? ☐

5. Does my supervisor, or someone at work, seem to care about me as a person? ☐

6. Is there someone at work who encourages my development? ☐

*M Buckingham & C Coffman, First Break all the Rules, Pocket Books 2005

# BUILDING ENGAGEMENT

|  | Score |
|---|---|
| 7. At work, do my opinions seem to count? | |
| 8. Does the mission/purpose of my company make me feel my job is important? | |
| 9. Are my co-workers committed to doing quality work? | |
| 10. Do I have a best friend at work? | |
| 11. In the last six months, has someone at work talked to me about my progress? | |
| 12. This last year, have I had opportunities at work to learn and grow? | |

*M Buckingham & C Coffman, First Break all the Rules, Pocket Books 2005

# THREE GOOD REASONS TO GET STARTED

If you want three good reasons for
developing your approach to
performance management
and engagement, remember
that it will help to:

1. Improve individual, team and organisational performance. ✔

2. Motivate, develop and release the potential of your people. ✔

3. Enable you to succeed in your role as manager of **performance**. ✔

# LEADING
# FOR PERFORMANCE

# THE IMPORTANCE OF LEADERSHIP

Leadership is critical to the achievement of high performance, no matter what your business or area of responsibility. It is also essential in helping others aspire to and attain high levels of performance for themselves and the organisation.

# HOW YOU SPEND YOUR TIME – EXERCISE

Think about your day at work and list down all the things that you do:

* _____

* _____

* _____

* _____

* _____

Now look at the next page and identify whether you have the right balance between **managing and leading**.

# HOW YOU SPEND YOUR TIME – ANALYSIS

**Managing**

- Emails
- Telephone calls
- Meetings
- Solving problems
- Writing reports
- Fire fighting

**Leading**

- Planning
- Communicating with the team
- Listening for ideas
- Supporting and coaching the team
- Delegating
- Providing feedback
- Influencing others

As you develop in your role it is important to focus more on leadership activities so that you can support your team to perform well.

LEADING FOR PERFORMANCE

# THE ENGAGING MANAGER – ARE YOU ONE?

A report from the Institute of Employment Studies* found that the leadership behaviours listed below were important in engaging others and delivering performance:

- Communicates – makes clear what is expected
- Listens, values and involves teams
- Is supportive and backs up the team
- Is target focused
- Shows empathy
- Has clear strategic vision
- Shows active interest in others
- Has good leadership skills
- Is respected
- Is able to deal with poor performance and deliver bad news

How would you rate yourself against this list?

*IES research – 2009

# ANALYSING YOUR COMPETENCIES

Leading for performance requires that you recognise both the transactional and the transformational aspects of leadership, to bring out the best in your people.

This questionnaire will help you to assess your leadership competencies. You can also give it to other people, to understand more about their perception of your leadership approach.

Please indicate the extent to which each of the statements on the following page applies to you. Think about each statement and rate yourself according to the 5-point scale below, where:

    5 = always
    4 = often
    3 = sometimes
    2 = rarely
    1 = never

LEADING FOR PERFORMANCE

# ANALYSING YOUR COMPETENCIES

## QUESTIONNAIRE

| | | |
|---|---|---|
| 1. | Listen carefully to others | 1 2 3 4 5 |
| 2. | Give people responsibility for tasks and projects | 1 2 3 4 5 |
| 3. | Challenge the rules and conventions in the organisation | 1 2 3 4 5 |
| 4. | Have a clear vision for the team | 1 2 3 4 5 |
| 5. | Have a clear perception of your strengths and weaknesses | 1 2 3 4 5 |
| 6. | Encourage ideas from the team | 1 2 3 4 5 |
| 7. | Demonstrate trust to others | 1 2 3 4 5 |
| 8. | Anticipate and adapt to changing conditions | 1 2 3 4 5 |
| 9. | Communicate the vision and ideas clearly to others | 1 2 3 4 5 |
| 10. | Spend time keeping up to date and developing new skills | 1 2 3 4 5 |
| 11. | Motivate and encourage others | 1 2 3 4 5 |
| 12. | Provide training to enable people to work effectively | 1 2 3 4 5 |
| 13. | Help others to manage change | 1 2 3 4 5 |
| 14. | Demonstrate a high level of commitment in your work | 1 2 3 4 5 |
| 15. | Manage time well | 1 2 3 4 5 |
| 16. | Develop a good communication network throughout the organisation | 1 2 3 4 5 |
| 17. | Provide support for people when needed | 1 2 3 4 5 |
| 18. | Manage stress well | 1 2 3 4 5 |
| 19. | Focus on achieving results | 1 2 3 4 5 |
| 20. | Have a positive attitude towards yourself | 1 2 3 4 5 |

# ANALYSING YOUR COMPETENCIES

## SCORING THE QUESTIONNAIRE

| Q | Column 1 score | Q | Column 2 score | Q | Column 3 score | Q | Column 4 score | Q | Column 5 score |
|---|---|---|---|---|---|---|---|---|---|
| 1 | | 2 | | 3 | | 4 | | 5 | |
| 6 | | 7 | | 8 | | 9 | | 10 | |
| 11 | | 12 | | 13 | | 14 | | 15 | |
| 16 | | 17 | | 18 | | 19 | | 20 | |
| Total | | Total | | Total | | Total | | Total | |

The leadership competencies contained in this questionnaire cover skills and behaviours associated with modern leadership, and can be classified under these headings:

Column 1 **L** istening
Column 2 **E** mpowering
Column 3 **A** dapting
Column 4 **D** elivering
Column 5 **S** elf-understanding

# LEADING FOR PERFORMANCE

## L.E.A.D.S.

Leading for performance means that you have to:

**L** isten          to others to understand their thoughts, concerns and aspirations

**E** mpower      others by giving them responsibility backed up by trust, training and support

**A** dapt          to changing situations and always be ready to listen to and implement new ideas

**D** eliver        high-quality results by setting clear goals and objectives which are linked to end results

**S** elf-understand   as the more you can understand yourself and your impact on others, the easier it is for you to manage yourself and adapt your style to bring out the best in others

# MANAGING YOUR OWN PERFORMANCE

To manage the performance of others, you need to:

- Be aware of your impact on others
- Be clear about your priorities
- Manage your time in a whole-life sense
- Manage your stress levels

> 'Your first and foremost job as a leader is to take charge of your own energy and then help orchestrate the energy of those around you.'
>
> **Peter F. Drucker**

## LEADING FOR PERFORMANCE

# UNDERSTANDING YOUR IMPACT ON OTHERS

To understand your impact on others:

- Gain feedback from friends and colleagues
- Use a 360° feedback questionnaire
- Analyse your strengths and weaknesses and compare them to other successful leaders in your organisation
- Find a mentor who can help you understand yourself
- Ask yourself what impression you and your office would give to a complete stranger

Through this process of feedback and reflection, think about:

- The impression you would like to make
- How you could adjust or adapt your approach to get the best out of yourself and others

# WORKING WITH YOUR STRENGTHS

Strengths are the 'underlying qualities that energise us, contribute to our personal growth and lead to peak performance'. (Brewerton and Brook, 2006)

They are personal sources of energy you can draw on:
- When the going is good
- In challenging times when you are under pressure
- To lead authentically
- To contribute to team and organisational goals

Working with your strengths has been shown to improve:
- Performance
- Engagement
- Resourcefulness and resilience
- Confidence

What are your strengths? It makes sense to focus on and develop them in your leadership role.

# RECOGNISE AN OVERUSED STRENGTH

One thing to be aware of is that an overused strength can become unproductive. For example, being achievement oriented is a positive strength, but overusing it might lead to pushing ideas through without consideration of others.

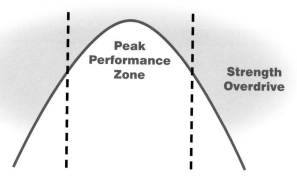

# IDENTIFY THE STRENGTHS IN OTHERS

Think about your team and list out their individual strengths. If you can help your team members to develop their strengths you will help them achieve a higher level of both individual and team performance.

| Team members | Strengths |
| --- | --- |
| • | |
| • | |
| • | |
| • | |
| • | |

# MANAGING YOUR STRESS LEVELS

When leading others it is important to recognise if you are feeling highly stressed. You won't be able to get the best out of your team if you are struggling personally.

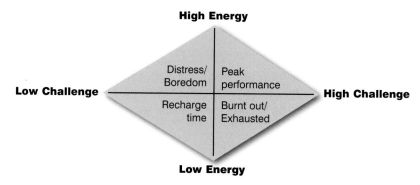

**High Energy**

Distress/ Boredom

Peak performance

**Low Challenge**

**High Challenge**

Recharge time

Burnt out/ Exhausted

**Low Energy**

# UNDERSTANDING STRESS LEVELS

| | |
|---|---|
| **Peak performance** | Your energy levels match the challenge at hand. Be aware that peak performance is not always sustainable over long periods of time. |
| **Burnt out** | Your energy levels do not match the challenge at hand – you are exhausted. |
| **Distress** | You are not being challenged. This can also cause stress. |
| **Recharge** | Recharge time is important at the end of each day to ensure that you have time for peace and relaxation. |

Where are you right now? Can you plan your life so that it has a good balance between energy and challenge, and can you build in some recharge time to help?

# TIPS FOR PERFORMING AT YOUR BEST

- Plan and prioritise your work
- Learn to say no
- Build breaks into your day
- Do some exercise
- Watch your caffeine intake
- Get some coaching – all top athletes have a coach
- Make sure you get sufficient sleep
- Monitor your working hours – no one can work effectively 24/7
- Make time for the people you work with
- Have some fun!

If you do this you will be working to your full potential and able to help your team to achieve as well.

LEADING FOR PERFORMANCE

# REVIEW & ACTIONS

In this section of the book we have looked at:

- The idea of managing less and leading more
- The LEADS model for analysing your leadership competencies
- Leadership and engagement
- The importance of self-understanding
- Recognising and working with your strengths
- Managing your stress levels

Identify three things you can take forward to develop your leadership approach:

1.

2.

3.

# PERFORMANCE MANAGEMENT SKILLS

# PERFORMANCE MANAGEMENT SKILLS

## OVERVIEW

Your role in helping team members to achieve their potential is an important one. This section looks at skills and techniques that will help you to work more effectively with others.

Rate your ability on a scale of 1 – 5 (where 5 = excellent and 1= in need of improvement). Also think about how often you use these skills. To build engagement and get the best from others you will need to give time to your team.

| Performance Management Skills | Rate Your Performance |
| --- | --- |
| Delegation | |
| Coaching | |
| Listening | |
| Asking questions | |
| Creating rapport | |
| Giving and receiving feedback | |
| Handling poor performance | |
| Motivation | |

# DELEGATING

## FIVE-STEP PROCESS

Delegation is often seen as a difficult area and, as a result, many managers use it less than they could. The five-step process for **planned delegation** provides a way of getting work done and also a way of motivating and developing people to bring in fresh ideas. This, in turn, will develop greater trust and a climate for success within the team.

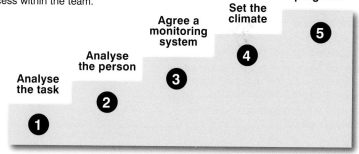

Analyse the task **1**

Analyse the person **2**

Agree a monitoring system **3**

Set the climate **4**

Review progress **5**

# PERFORMANCE MANAGEMENT SKILLS

## DELEGATING

### STEP 1: ANALYSE THE TASK

- Identify tasks you are unlikely to complete on your own and mark a portion or all of them for delegation
- Are there any longer-term projects you could delegate in development stage?
- Will the task provide the person with some sort of challenge or are you just dumping?
- Who else will you need to inform if you are delegating a task which involves others?
- How can you ensure that the individual will have the right degree of authority and responsibility to achieve the task?
- Can you link delegation to coaching and development?

This diagram may help you identify which tasks can be delegated, by looking at which quadrant they fit into.

# PERFORMANCE MANAGEMENT SKILLS

## **DELEGATING**

### STEP 2: ANALYSE THE PERSON

- Who are the team members most suitable for delegation?

- What workload do they have? Do they have the resources, knowledge and skills to achieve the task?

- Will it dovetail into work they are already doing?

- What's in it for them? Will it help their development, provide them with greater visibility or provide a coaching opportunity?

Try to stretch people but don't break them. The challenges provided by delegation can be motivational but, if handled badly, can be stressful and threatening.

PERFORMANCE MANAGEMENT SKILLS

# DELEGATING
## STEP 3: AGREE A MONITORING SYSTEM

- Involve the individual in the setting up of the monitoring system
- Agree goals and targets for what you want to achieve by when
- You may need to break the task down into stages or sub-tasks
- Both parties need to be clear about what is being delegated and what is not
- Define clear success criteria so that you both know what quality standards are required and what the end result should look like
- Agree times to review progress; this will vary according to the task and the confidence of the individual

PERFORMANCE MANAGEMENT SKILLS

# DELEGATING

## STEP 4: SET THE CLIMATE FOR DELEGATION

- Listen to ideas from the person to whom you are delegating; he or she will often bring a fresh perspective to the situation

- Keep the communication channels open at all times so the person can approach you if problems are encountered

- Build in praise and feedback along the way so that the individual feels appreciated, and ensure that credit is given for the work done

- Don't interfere between review periods; you need to build trust and show that you can empower the individual

- Build in coaching and development opportunities where necessary so the person has the skills and abilities to complete the task

PERFORMANCE MANAGEMENT SKILLS

# DELEGATING

## STEP 5: REVIEW PROGRESS

- Review progress on a regular basis
- Provide support and guidance
- Ask searching questions to help the individual think things through rather than provide all the answers
- When the task is completed review the progress against the success criteria you set earlier
- Review the learning, identifying any new skills and competencies that have been acquired and any new learning goals for the future
- Gain feedback on your role; consider if there is anything else you could do in the future to improve your delegation

# COACHING

Coaching involves helping individuals or teams to develop and reach their full potential. Coaching usually takes place at work. There may be a task that you, as manager, need to delegate or something you currently do which could be a learning opportunity for someone else. It may be something looming in the future, a project or a presentation which would provide a developmental challenge to one of your team.

It is also important to focus on the people you wish to coach:

- What do they need to do to develop further?
- Do they have a performance gap?
- Is there something they do well which you could build on?

41

# THE COACHING PROCESS

Matching the needs of the manager with those of the individual being coached requires careful planning. This can be agreed and developed during the initial coaching meeting.

**Agree the development need**

**Identify and agree a suitable project**

**Agree the task and learning outcomes**

**Identify a process of review, follow-up, feedback and support**

**Ensure that the individual is given the right degree of responsibility and authority to complete the task**

**Monitor progress and review the results**

# PERFORMANCE MANAGEMENT SKILLS

## COACHING SKILLS

Coaching requires managers to use a whole range of skills. They need to be aware of:

- Their own approach and influence on the people they are coaching
- The style and needs of those being coached; this means thinking about:
  - their development needs
  - the way they learn best
  - possible pitfalls and problems

In addition, managers need to hone four key skills in order to coach effectively.
These are:

1. Listening     2. Questioning     3. Rapport     4. Feedback

# COACHING SKILLS: LISTENING

**L** Look at the learner; use good eye contact and open body language to show you are listening

**I** Interruptions - avoid them so you can give 100% of your attention

**S** Summarise regularly so that you are both clear about what you have agreed and how you will progress with the coaching project

**T** Time - allow sufficient; coaching requires regular meetings to monitor and review progress

**E** Encourage the person to talk and come up with options and ideas to move the project forward

**N** Nurture an environment of trust where the individual can feel free to contribute and ask questions which they know will be dealt with in an objective and supportive manner

# COACHING SKILLS: LISTENING

In coaching, you need to listen not only to the thoughts and ideas being spoken but also to the feelings and emotions being expressed and the intentions and commitment the learner has to the issue at hand.

**Listening to <u>thoughts</u> requires:**

- Listening to **all** the words that are being spoken; we often listen selectively and get side-tracked on issues which are of more importance to us
- Identifying the data that the learner has collected and used
- Understanding the learner's approach and logic in working the issue through
- Summarising and using the learner's words to reflect back his or her ideas and thoughts

# COACHING SKILLS: LISTENING

**Listening to <u>feelings</u> requires:**
- Listening to the way in which the learner presents his or her ideas
- Asking yourself:
    - Is their tone confident or concerned?
    - Is their body language positive and open, or defensive and closed?
    - Is their eye contact clear and direct, or shifting and avoiding?
    - Is the pace fast, or slow and faltering?

**Listening to <u>intentions</u> requires:**
- Listening to what the learner intends to do about the situation
- Establishing what the learner's conclusions and judgements are about the situation
- Identifying what the learner wants
- Measuring the level of the learner's commitment

Good listening, therefore, requires that you listen with all your senses. Using the skills effectively can pay real dividends.

# COACHING SKILLS: QUESTIONING

Asking questions is an important area of coaching.
Questions can be used to:

- Help the learner develop ideas

- Explore all the options available

- Encourage the learner to think through all the issues

- Help the learner take ownership for the coaching project

- Motivate the learner further, as the individual realises that he or she has the ability to complete the task

# COACHING SKILLS: QUESTIONING

We often focus on what is wrong and what isn't working with questions such as:

- What is your problem?
- How long have you had it?
- Who's to blame?
- Why haven't you solved it?
- What will you do about it?

It's much more positive to focus on outcomes and what can be achieved with questions such as:

- What do you want?
- How will you know when you have achieved it?
- What else will you improve?
- What resources do you already have?
- Is there something similar in which you have already succeeded?
- What's the next step?

## PERFORMANCE MANAGEMENT SKILLS

# COACHING SKILLS: G.R.O.W. MODEL

The **G.R.O.W.** model is a questioning approach to coaching which builds on positive questioning.

The model guides the coach to ask the learners questions about:

**G**oals     Are they clear about what they want to achieve?
Have they set any sub-goals along the way?
Are the goals realistic and measurable?

**R**eality     Where are they right now with the project?
What is helping or hindering the process?
Is there anyone they can learn from?

**O**ptions     What are the options available?
Are there any other possibilities?
Which is the most appropriate option?

**W**ill     What is their level of commitment?
If commitment is low, would they be better off focusing their energy elsewhere?
What would be the consequences of this?

*Adapted from 'Coaching for Performance', John Whitmore, Nicholas Brealey, 2009.*

Goals → Reality → Options → Will (cycle diagram)

# COACHING SKILLS: CREATING RAPPORT

If you can create a good level of rapport when coaching, it will be easier to develop empathy and create an environment of trust.

Rapport has three main elements:

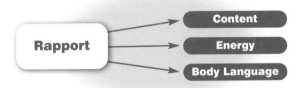

# COACHING SKILLS: CREATING RAPPORT

**Content** Find an area of common ground to talk about. If you are talking about something you are both familiar with, you will develop rapport.

**Energy** Some people are generally faster-paced than others. They will talk faster, use more body movements, and have more variety of tone in their voice. Other people are slower-paced. They are more thoughtful in their approach. To develop rapport it is important to match the other person's style.

**Body language** Do some people-watching. You will notice that often people who are in conversation sit in the same way, use the same hand actions and literally 'mirror each other'. This doesn't mean copying the other person, but it helps to be aware of their body language and use a similar approach.

As a coach you need to create rapport – the chances are it will happen naturally but these are a few pointers to help you on the way.

# COACHING SKILLS: GIVING FEEDBACK

Feedback is essential throughout the coaching process for both the coach and the learner. The coaches will benefit from feedback on their role and the learners will require feedback to know how they are progressing, what they are doing well and where they could improve. A useful way of thinking about feedback is to use **BOOST**:

**B**alance      Include positive elements as well as reflecting on areas for improvement.

**O**bserved     What you have seen them do; focus on behaviour not personality.

**O**wnership    Both parties must own the feedback for it to be useful and actionable.

**S**pecific     Try to keep the feedback specific and factual so that it is clear and understandable.

**T**ime         Pick the appropriate time to give feedback and give it in an atmosphere of trust.

It is often best to start by asking those concerned how they think they are doing - they will usually be very honest about their performance and you will only have to add to or confirm their ideas.

# COACHING SKILLS: RECEIVING FEEDBACK

For anyone receiving feedback, it can be a difficult process. Remember:

- Don't get defensive
- Ask questions to clarify the feedback and explore the issue further
- Don't ignore praise; take it on board
- It's your choice to accept or reject the feedback offered
- Work out what you can do with the feedback, how it can help you to improve your performance
- Remember to say thank you (feedback is not always easy to deliver)

# POOR PERFORMANCE

We all have people who are not performing to standard, but try not to label them as 'poor' performers. Over their careers, people may have times when they are performing well and other times when they are not bringing in the results you expect. Your challenge is to maintain and develop the performance of all your people.

One of the main issues is when to act. Managing poor performance is a bit like catching sand falling through an hourglass. You need to tackle the grains rather than wait for a heap of sand to build up.

# GET TO THE ROOT OF THE PROBLEM

It's really important to explore the cause of the performance issue, and only by talking about the situation will you be able to work out how to tackle it together.

their ability

your ability

process gap

motivation

personal issues

environment

# GET TO THE ROOT OF THE PROBLEM

There may be a number of reasons for the poor performance.

1. **Personal ability:** Has the individual the capability? Is there a skills gap needing training?

2. **Manager ability:** Have I given enough direction, and made sufficient resources available?

3. **Process gap:** Has the appraisal system been at fault? Have the goalposts moved or external forces made the task unattainable? Have there been regular enough review sessions and is the reward system pointing in the right direction?

4. **Environmental forces:** Has the organisation created departmental barriers, red-tape overkill, cultural restrictions or hidden agendas which make the task impossible?

5. **Personal circumstances:** Has something at home affected performance at work?

6. **Motivation:** Is the person demotivated or suffering from stress or lack of challenge?

Poor performance can often be a symptom of other problems. Obviously, you need to work with the individual concerned to recognise where the problem is and how it should be resolved.

## PERFORMANCE MANAGEMENT SKILLS

# DEALING WITH POOR PERFORMANCE

- Discuss the issue, providing clear feedback and explaining the consequences of continued poor performance

- Try to get to the root of the issue; establish the real cause of the poor performance

- Explore all the options and alternatives available to help bring the person back on track

- Agree the next steps and set clear objectives for improvements; establish regular review meetings to monitor progress

- Provide training and coaching if appropriate

- Monitor and document progress; several short-term hiccups may point to a more deep-seated problem requiring firmer action

**Catching performance issues in time can lead to improved individual and team performance.**

# CREATE A PERFORMANCE PLAN

A performance improvement plan is there to help turn the performance issue around. It should be developed with the individual and it should contain:

- Some clear measurable objectives related to the issue
- Regular review dates where progress and feedback can be recorded
- Coaching and training where appropriate, to support the improvement

You will need to set times for regular feedback sessions so that you can monitor progress. Your aim is to bring the performance back up to standard and ensure that it is maintained in the future.

PERFORMANCE MANAGEMENT SKILLS

# DIFFICULT CONVERSATIONS – BOFF

It's very important to prepare well for conversations that tackle areas such as performance and it is something that managers often put off. This framework may help you to get your message across clearly.

BOFF stands for:

**B**ehaviour – Describe the behaviour

**O**utcome – Explain the outcome and result of the behaviour

**F**eelings – Explain how this makes you feel

**F**uture – Explore what can be done to make sure the situation changes

## DIFFICULT CONVERSATIONS – BOFF

### EXAMPLE

Anysha was feeling frustrated. Each week one of her team members Sunil prepared the weekly financial report. However it was often full of mistakes and Anysha spent her weekends making corrections in time for the management meeting on Monday. She had raised the issue with Sunil on a number of occasions and despite extra coaching and training he still made mistakes.

Think about how you could use the BOFF model to help Anysha manage the conversation.

PERFORMANCE MANAGEMENT SKILLS

# DIFFICULT CONVERSATIONS – BOFF
SOLUTION

Using the BOFF model to prepare for the conversation Anysha could think about the following conversation.

Sunil, I've noticed that there were five major mistakes in this week's financial report. (**Behaviour**)

It meant I had to work over the weekend to make sure the report was acceptable for the Monday meeting. (**Outcome**)

I'm really concerned (**Feeling**) as this is not the first time the situation has occurred.

What can we do to make sure that next week's figures are 100% accurate? (**Future**)

PERFORMANCE MANAGEMENT SKILLS

# MOTIVATING

There is a whole range of motivational theories but the secret to motivation is to understand your people.

- People are motivated by different things at different stages of their lives
- You have a greater influence than you may realise in motivating your people

In surveys by the American Psychological Association, half of all employees who said they did not feel valued at work also said that they intend to look for a new job next year.

The research also showed that employees who felt valued are likely to have better physical and mental health and higher levels of engagement, satisfaction and motivation. *(Business News 2012).*

The role of motivation is directly linked to performance and your role as a manager has a direct impact on whether your people feel valued and engaged.

# THINK ABOUT YOUR PEOPLE

Different people are motivated by different things. Look at the people in your team and try to identify what it is that motivates them.

Here are a few ideas to help you think about the personalities in your team:

**Achievers** – are never happier than when they have a goal to chase. They will be motivated by challenge. They will like to have targets and be given the freedom to succeed.

**Analysts** – are motivated by getting to the truth. They will appreciate time to focus on the task at hand and work with the data. Their motivation is to achieve an accurate result.

**Responders** – these people respond to praise and feedback. You will notice them as they will often ask for feedback and let you know what they have done. Knowing they are appreciated and doing a good job is their main motivator.

Brilliant

Well done!

PERFORMANCE MANAGEMENT SKILLS

# THINK ABOUT YOUR PEOPLE

**Team players** – enjoy working with others to achieve results. They will be motivated by their role in the team and the support and input they can contribute to the team.

**Materialists** – these people are motivated by the material things their work can provide and will be motivated by hitting financial targets and claiming their just reward.

**Developers** – are motivated by self-development. They will love the opportunity to learn new things either through their job or on external training programmes. Their motivation is to continually grow and they will get bored with routine tasks.

Your challenge is to recognise what motivates your people and where possible adjust your style to meet their preference.

PERFORMANCE MANAGEMENT SKILLS

# RESEARCH FINDINGS

Research shows that there is some difference between what managers say motivates them and what organisations rely on. So don't make assumptions about motivation. Check with your team and remember there is a lot you can do as a manager to motivate them. (Ashridge Management Index 2009)

| What managers want (Ranking) | | What organisations rely on (Ranking) |
|:---:|:---|:---:|
| 1 | Challenging/interesting work | 2 |
| 2 | Opportunity to continually learn and develop skills and knowledge | 5 |
| 3 | A high basic salary | 6 |
| 4 | The authority to run 'my own show' | 15 |
| 5 | Clear career advancement within the organisation | 8 |
| 6 | Knowing my decisions have an impact on the organisation | 14 |
| 7 | Performance related pay/incentive schemes | 1 |

# PERFORMANCE MANAGEMENT SKILLS

## REVIEW & ACTIONS

In this section we have looked at:

- How to delegate
- The skills of coaching
- Listening at different levels
- Turning around poor performance
- Handling difficult conversations
- Your role in helping to motivate team members

List three things you have found useful and can use in your job:

1. _____

2. _____

3. _____

# PERFORMANCE MANAGEMENT PROCESS

# PERFORMANCE REVIEWS

Performance reviews are often seen as an extra burden. Yet, if managed well, they can be a positive and useful process providing you, the manager, and your people with the opportunity to discuss issues such as:

- Achievements over the past year
- Their current performance
- Objectives which will be set for next year
- Personal learning and development needs
- Longer-term career prospects
- Skills and experience which they are perhaps under-using

The real success of any appraisal lies in the interaction between the appraiser and appraisee and establishing a relationship that can be built upon throughout the year.
The performance review process can be divided into three stages:

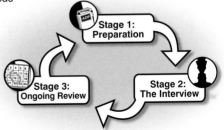

Stage 1:
Preparation

Stage 2:
The Interview

Stage 3:
Ongoing Review

# PERFORMANCE REVIEWS

## STAGE 1: PREPARATION

Don't overlook the amount of time and effort you will need to give to the preparation to ensure a worthwhile appraisal.

- Make sure you have set aside enough time

- Make sure that you will be free from interruptions

- Ensure that the room layout is conducive to a relaxed one-to-one meeting

- Give plenty of notice to the appraisees so that they have time to prepare

- Spend time collecting the relevant data; this may involve talking to internal or external customers to obtain a valid view of their overall performance

- Finally, both parties need to prepare the relevant paperwork and review last year's objectives; this is an important process as it allows time to think through all the appropriate performance issues and provides a checklist of points to cover

# PERFORMANCE REVIEWS

### STAGE 2: THE INTERVIEW

The interview is the most important part of the process. If handled well, it is a valuable motivational and planning tool for the year ahead.

- Ensure that you spend some time putting the appraisee at ease
- Ask questions to encourage self-analysis
- Ensure that the meeting is a two-way process; this involves listening and exploring the appraisee's views and ideas
- Give helpful feedback which involves praising the good things but not ignoring areas of poor performance
- Spend time looking at the appraisee's performance during the year and then look ahead to the new goals and objectives which need to be set
- Make sure that you have also looked at development needs for the coming period and helped the appraisee think about how to develop him/herself for the future
- Try to let the appraisee summarise the discussion and make sure that you record all the agreements and action steps
- At the end of the appraisal interview, there is usually a certain amount of paperwork which needs to be completed; ensure that you allow enough time to do this

PERFORMANCE MANAGEMENT PROCESS

# PERFORMANCE REVIEWS
STAGE 3: ONGOING REVIEW

The appraisal interview is just one part of the whole performance review cycle. Appraising performance should be ongoing and include:

**Regular feedback**  People need to know how they are progressing and time should be set aside to communicate this with them. This means that at the next appraisal meeting you really can observe the 'law of no surprises'.

**Ongoing coaching**  This is an excellent way of helping individuals to develop through their work. Coaching projects can be set up as part of an individual's development plan. Interim meetings will also ensure that objectives are being met and that the individual is aware of their performance and progress and also of any change in terms of their targets and objectives.

**Development and training**  These activities need to go on throughout the year so that the individual is equipped with the skills to do his or her job and to develop into new roles.

Remember, the performance appraisal process can be rewarding and genuinely helpful to both parties, by formalising an evaluation of the previous year's work and planning ahead for the next.

# OBJECTIVE SETTING FOR RESULTS

Objectives need to be set at all levels of the business. This ensures commitment at the higher levels of management and clear goals and objectives at lower levels. This is often achieved through cascading the corporate or strategic objectives into individual jobs.

CORPORATE or STRATEGIC PLANS

BUSINESS PLANS

DEPARTMENTAL GOALS

TEAM GOALS

INDIVIDUAL OBJECTIVES

# PERFORMANCE MANAGEMENT PROCESS

## CHANGES IN OBJECTIVE SETTING

The focus on objective setting has changed with the growing complexity and pace of everyday work.

| From | To |
|------|-----|
| Objectives are set on an annual basis | Objectives are likely to change during the year |
| Reviews are held twice a year | Performance is reviewed on a regular basis |
| Focus on measurable hard objectives | Focus on hard and soft objectives |
| Focus on the job | Focus on the role and whole person |
| Focus on activities | Focus on outcomes |
| Focus on achievements | Focus on future development |
| Feedback comes directly from the manager | Feedback comes from multiple sources |

# OBJECTIVES FOR GOOD OBJECTIVES

### Linked to business priorities
The cascade approach described on page 72 links jobs at all levels.
Objectives must be regularly reviewed and updated as circumstances change.

### Linked to results, not activities
This means that we are concerned with output not activities - the ends and not
the means.

### Measurable and specific
Objectives must state what exactly is to be measured, and within that, define acceptable
levels of performance.

### Challenging but attainable
Ideally, your people should set their own objectives. Often these will be tougher than if
set by the manager. They should be stretching, challenging and developmental. Weed
out unattainable objectives as these can be demotivating.

# OBJECTIVES FOR GOOD OBJECTIVES

**Matching experience and capability**  Objectives should take account of the individual's ability, experience, knowledge and any development plan in place.

**Updated**  Certain things may occur which affect the objective being measured but which are out of the control of the jobholder. As a result, objectives must be regularly updated, taking account of the business environment.

**Number of objectives**  Don't set too many objectives. It is better to focus on a few quality areas rather than a long list which is impossible to achieve.

**Compatible upwards/downwards/sideways**  Objectives should not clash with other people's activities, so they need to be compatible upwards, downwards and sideways.

*A software manufacturer has two departments sitting next to each other. The first department is responsible for developing new software and has target dates for issuing the product. The second department is responsible for quality and has objectives relating to customer complaints on use of the software. It is easy to see that the two departments have conflicting objectives and there is a potential for bad feeling as one department frustrates the other's objectives.*

# HARD & SOFT OBJECTIVES

Hard objectives can be measured clearly in terms of outputs such as turnover, profit, percentage increases, etc. Soft objectives define the difference between 'acceptable' and 'excellent' performance. Soft objectives cover areas where **the way the job is done** is as important as the quantitative results.

*A hotel receptionist may be measured only in terms of the number of guests booked into and checked out of the hotel each day, and the ability to answer the phone within three rings. These would be the hard objectives. How welcome the guests felt and the telephone manner used are obviously key to the hotel's success. These would make up the soft objectives, more difficult to measure, owing to their qualitative nature, but very important nonetheless.*

Often soft objectives are measured through:
- Customer feedback
- Surveys
- Complaints
- Mystery shoppers

However, these are not always personalised.

# DEFINING SOFT OBJECTIVES

It is important to break down soft objectives into desirable behaviours, ie: a positive attitude for a hotel receptionist tells you little until it is broken down into:

- Politeness
- Smiling and good eye contact with the customer at all times
- Appearance as described in the handbook
- Calm and practical approach
- Good knowledge of the hotel's services and systems

The real secret with soft objectives is that even if they can't be measured in the strictest sense, they can always be described. Once you have a clear picture, it is easier to train, develop and provide specific feedback to each individual involved.

PERFORMANCE MANAGEMENT PROCESS

# SELF-DEVELOPMENT OBJECTIVES

People need to focus on their own development - expanding their repertoire of skills in preparation for future assignments and opportunities. Development objectives can range from:

- Coaching projects
- Assignments which will develop a specific skill or ability
- Courses offered by the organisation or other providers
- Activities outside work which will aid development
- Self-study activities

Ideally, people should have at least one self-development objective per year.

PERFORMANCE MANAGEMENT PROCESS

# SELF-DEVELOPMENT OBJECTIVES
EXAMPLES

*Jo needed to learn how to deal with a broad range of people and, in particular, break tasks and instructions down into understandable terms. She negotiated with her employer to spend one afternoon per month teaching economics to secondary school pupils. This helped her to acquire the patience and skills to be able to clearly explain issues and tasks in the workplace.*

*John attended evening class to understand more about information technology and systems. He worked in a warehouse as a packer but recognised that IT skills were essential for the future.*

*Sue took on a role as school governor as a way of contributing to the community, but also developed her wider management skills.*

*Pat took on the role of organising a major sales conference for her company. This increased her network and profile amongst colleagues and clients, and developed her confidence and her skills in managing projects.*

# MEASURING PERFORMANCE

Objectives help you measure performance but **beware**:

- Are you measuring the right thing? Remember: what gets measured gets managed, but what gets measured is often what is easy to measure.
- Are there too many measures on which to focus?
- Are you using measurement in a negative, punitive way?
- Do people understand how the measures fit into the bigger picture?
- Are measures imposed or do employees have an input into the process?
- Are individual measures appropriate or would team measures be more suitable?
- Do you review and change measures as business priorities change?

# TEAM-BASED MEASURES

If you wish to enhance team performance, develop some team measure (the team is usually best placed to do this). Measures can be set around:

- The overall objectives and targets for the team
- Quality objectives
- Customer satisfaction targets
- Absenteeism
- Skill levels for the team

It is important that individual and team objectives don't work against each other but complement the bigger picture. And, remember to celebrate team success!

# BALANCED BUSINESS SCORECARD

Many organisations are trying to find ways of looking at performance measurement from a whole-business point of view. What a job-holder does in the short-term needs to tie in with long-term organisational goals, and understanding the linkage is the key to successful performance management.

The Balanced Business Scorecard (BBS) framework does just this, translating the organisation's vision into understandable objectives at every level in the organisation. It provides an instant snapshot of performance in four key areas, as the diagram shows. The same areas apply across both organisations and departments within organisations.

**FINANCIAL PERSPECTIVE**
How do we look to our stakeholders?

**CUSTOMER PERSPECTIVE**
How does our organisation look to our customers?

**Business Strategy**

**ORGANISATION LEARNING**
Are we able to sustain innovations, change and improve?

**PROCESS PERSPECTIVE**
How effective are our key business processes?

82

PERFORMANCE MANAGEMENT PROCESS

# BALANCED BUSINESS SCORECARD

TIPS

- Measures in each area will vary depending on the particular organisation and its mission; in turn, these will vary according to the level being examined:
    - the BBS for a business unit will have measures relating to the organisation's mission
    - the BBS for a team will relate to the team's goals
    - the BBS for an individual will focus on that person's objectives
- Balance is the keyword: each area is equally important and there should be no more than four or five measures in each of the quadrants (try not to measure everything and lose focus in a myriad of targets)
- Involve people from across the organisation to develop measures
- The chosen measures must reflect the culture of the organisation (Are you people driven or technology driven? Do you measure product innovations or job satisfaction?) The messages to the employees will depend on the measures used

# CREATING YOUR OWN SCORECARD

You can create your own scorecard with your team.
First, you need to be clear about your team vision
and goals; then develop quadrants and
measures to support them.

| Vision | Goals |
|--------|-------|

# COMPLETED SCORECARD

Here is an example of a scorecard, completed for an IT department.

**Vision**
Provide the most effective and efficient IT solutions for the organisation

**Goals**
- Customer satisfaction
- Clear IT strategy
- Well-trained team
- Work within budget

**Customer Satisfaction**
- Reduce Stress
- Monitor Service
- Response Time
- Benchmarking

**Business Focus**
- IT Strategy
- Progress Review
- Business Application
- Managing Infrastructure

**Team Learning**
- Adequate Training
- Skills Audit
- Team Coaching
- Review Meetings

**Financial**
- Contractor Costs
- Software
- Capital Costs
- Outsourcing

The IT manager used the Balanced Business Scorecard to create objectives and measures for the team which fed directly into the team goals, vision and overall business objectives.

# PERFORMANCE MANAGEMENT PROCESS

## REVIEW & ACTIONS

In this section we have looked at:

- The role of performance reviews
- Conducting an appraisal meeting
- Setting hard and soft objectives
- Measuring performance
- The balanced scorecard and how to use it

List three things you have found useful and can use in your job:

1. _____

2. _____

3. _____

# CREATING HIGH-PERFORMING TEAMS

# CREATING HIGH-PERFORMING TEAMS

# TEAMWORK IS IMPORTANT

We all work in teams. Some we see every day and others we communicate with via the internet, yet all are important to our success.

Think about the number of teams you are in:

- What is your role in each team?
- How effective are the different teams?
- What are the characteristics of the most effective teams?

We need to understand what makes good teamwork and replicate it elsewhere.

# TEAMWORK IS IMPORTANT

Teamwork is vitally important. If teams are developed to perform well, they can:

- **Improve quality and productivity** – teams can set up and monitor processes and be mutually accountable for the results

- **Improve service** – a unified and consistent approach to service means that the whole team can focus on meeting customer needs

- **Decrease operating costs** – by improving productivity and workflow, bottom line benefits are realised

- **Encourage motivation and creativity** – teams often know best how to improve the way they work

- **Simplify job structures** – team members can support each other

# WHY TEAMS FAIL

If teams fail, it is often a result of one or more of the following:

| | |
|---|---|
| **Lack of support** | If there is no support and encouragement from above, team morale will fade. |
| **No clear purpose** | Teams need clear goals and purpose so they know where they are going. |
| **No team structure** | Teams need structures and processes to manage their performance, ie: regular reviews, feedback systems and mechanisms for problem-solving. |
| **Inappropriate systems** | Performance management systems which encourage and reward individual performance can be detrimental to team performance. |
| **Group think** | Lack of diversity and a similarity in approaches and styles can prevent new ideas being introduced. |
| **Hidden agendas** | Are usually private and not declared and can prevent the team from moving ahead. |
| **Conflicting views** | Conflict can hold the team back but, if resolved, can lead to a collaborative approach. |
| **Dominant v quiet members** | All team members need to be involved for a team to work effectively. |

# STAGES OF TEAM DEVELOPMENT

There are four stages of development which teams move through in order to achieve high performance:

1. **Forming** – when a team initially comes together.

2. **Storming** – often a difficult time when the team is working out roles and responsibilities.

3. **Norming** – involves setting rules and finding ways of working together. These give the team some identity and make the individuals more comfortable about the group.

4. **Performing** – once the rough edges have been knocked off the group and they have found a way of working together, they can really perform and take on the challenge of working together as a team.

*Adapted from B.W Tuckman (1965) Development Sequence in small groups, Psychological Bulletin, 63, 284-499*

# WHAT DO HIGH-PERFORMING TEAMS DO?

When a team is performing really well, the members:

- Set high output and high quality targets
- Achieve targets and celebrate success
- Understand each other and appreciate differences
- Respect each other
- Are balanced in terms of the roles and skills they bring to the team
- Have responsibility and autonomy to achieve the results
- Are client orientated
- Regularly review and improve their performance
- Enjoy working together and are motivated to achieve

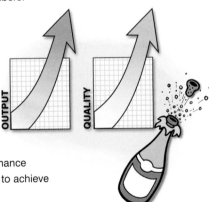

# TASK, PROCESS & RELATIONSHIPS

When leading a team you need to focus on three elements:

- The task
- The process (how you work together)
- The relationships (the way you work together)

Managers often focus the majority of their time and attention on the task and don't think enough about how the team should work together and how to build strong working relationships. This can cause difficulties and result in reduced team efficiency.

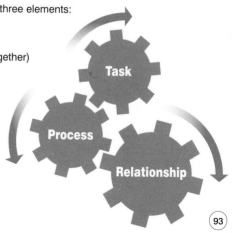

CREATING HIGH-PERFORMING TEAMS

# TEAM EFFECTIVENESS QUESTIONNAIRE

Use the questionnaire that follows to find out if your team is performing at its best. There are five areas to look at:

1. **Purpose** – Is it clear, understood and taken on with enthusiasm by members of the team?

2. **Performance** – Do the team members quantify their performance and are they happy with the results?

3. **Relationships** – Does everyone know, or at least appreciate, what each is bringing to the team and are the different roles recognised?

4. **Communication** – Are people listening to each other and do they feel confident enough to put forward their own views?

5. **Learning** – Does any individual or the whole team need more skills to work effectively?

You can give the questionnaire to members of your team to discover their views.

# CREATING HIGH-PERFORMING TEAMS

 **TEAM EFFECTIVENESS QUESTIONNAIRE**

How would you rate your team on a scale of 1 - 5 (1 = not at all, 5 = very true)?

| | | |
|---|---|---|
| **Purpose** | We are committed to a common purpose | |
| | Our goals are clear, challenging and relevant | |
| | The purpose is aligned to the organisational strategy | |
| **Performance** | We know how we are doing | |
| | We get rewarded for achieving results | |
| | We know what the targets are and they're SMART | |
| **Relationships** | We get on really well | |
| | Each one of us is individually accountable | |
| | We bring different skills but each person's role is respected | |

# CREATING HIGH-PERFORMING TEAMS

 ## TEAM EFFECTIVENESS QUESTIONNAIRE

| | | |
|---|---|---|
| **Communication** | We all express ourselves openly and honestly while the others listen | |
| | We brainstorm and explore different ideas | |
| | We communicate well with the wider organisation | |
| **Learning** | Whenever we see a need, we arrange training | |
| | If necessary, we coach each other in certain areas | |
| | We review the team process and recognise our accomplishments | |

What is the team really good at? What don't we do well? What can we do to improve?

# RUNNING A TEAM SESSION

If you have to run a team meeting, always try to ensure that the creativity and ideas of the team are included. You will need to think about how to use the meeting to get the most out of the team and the following tips may help.

- Let the team members have a chance to catch up with each other. Share progress and successes and use it as an opportunity to show your appreciation for their work

- Introduce the discussion topic with background information (give the team prior notice of this so they have a chance to develop their ideas)

- Make sure everyone has a chance to voice his or her opinion. Use techniques such as brainstorming or buzz groups to generate ideas and bring in quieter members of the team. Keep an eye on the body language of the group, checking for signs of impatience, boredom, apathy and enthusiasm

CREATING HIGH-PERFORMING TEAMS

# RUNNING A TEAM SESSION

- Summarise the thoughts of the group and check this is correct

- Specify what decisions have been made and what actions will now occur. These may need documenting and circulating so people are clear what needs to be done and by when

- Check if there is any unfinished business or other topics which need raising

- Review the process of the group. What went well, not so well? How are the people feeling right now? What could be improved on for the next meeting?

In this way, you are managing not only the task issues in the meeting but also the process issues which lead to good teamwork.

CREATING HIGH-PERFORMING TEAMS

# DO'S & DON'TS OF FACILITATING

| DO | DON'T |
|---|---|
| Prepare | Wing it |
| Keep a check on time | Let things run away |
| Use voice and body language to encourage ideas and show that you are listening | Use your position and power to push through your own agenda |
| Build on others' contributions | Shoot down ideas too readily |
| Get all relevant opinions | Take sides |
| Keep control of the discussion but allow all ideas to be heard | Be manipulative, condescending or dismissive |
| Generate enthusiasm | Appear tired of it all |
| Summarise and conclude | Leave things for next time |
| Review the process and agree on any improvements | Carry on with processes which are not producing the best results |
| Think about developing team members so that they can facilitate future meetings | Create an expectation that you will always drive the process |

# CREATING HIGH-PERFORMING TEAMS

## BUILDING TRUST IN YOUR TEAM

Trust is a very important ingredient in achieving a high level of team performance. The diagram below shows the relationship between trust and project effectiveness.

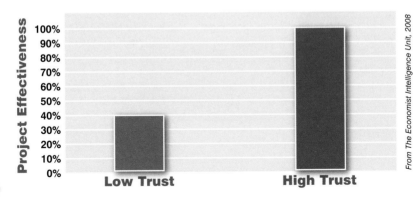

*From The Economist Intelligence Unit, 2008*

CREATING HIGH-PERFORMING TEAMS

# BUILDING TRUST IN YOUR TEAM

Here are some tips for building trust in your team:

- Communicate through regular newsletters and updates
- Support a common cause – a charity or sports team
- Celebrate success, birthdays, leaving do's – virtual parties!
- Create a positive climate through your actions: 'model the way'
- Team training – do it together
- Make sure people's roles are clear
- Make sure everyone keeps their commitments to the team
- Use some psychometrics to get to know each other's preferences
- Build on strengths and give praise
- When you do get together plan for plenty of social time and facilitate the meeting to build relationships

# HOW COMPLEX IS YOUR TEAM

Often the teams we work in are very complex. Look at the table below and think about your team. How complex is it? If you can tick three or more boxes it's a complex one. You may need to give special attention to how you communicate and work with team members, especially if you are working virtually or across cultures.

| | |
|---|---|
| **Multicultural** | ◯ |
| **Multidisciplinary** | ◯ |
| **Multigenerational** | ◯ |
| **Geographically dispersed** | ◯ |
| **Working across time zones** | ◯ |
| **Virtual (rarely meeting up)** | ◯ |
| **Working in partnership with other organisations** | ◯ |

CREATING HIGH-PERFORMING TEAMS

# WORKING AT A DISTANCE – VIRTUAL COMMUNUICATION

When you are working at a distance, traditional face-to-face communication is replaced by telephone and email, so it's important to develop your non-visual skills.

- Listen for tone, intonation, pace, use of words
- Listen to what is not said
- Ask lots of open questions
- Check for understanding
- Summarise
- Involve others – make sure everyone communicates
- 'Mine for conflict' – it can only be dealt with when it's out in the open
- Work on your cross cultural awareness
- Make sure you create a positive tone in your emails
- Keep emails clear, polite, short and action-oriented

# WORKING AT A DISTANCE – COMMUNICATION STRATEGY

When you have little opportunity to meet up as a team a good communication strategy will help all the individual members feel included.

Paula led a team spread across four countries, five locations. Three of the team spoke English as their second language. As part of her communication strategy she planned:

- A major team meeting each year, with some social time
- A weekly webex meeting where people could update each other and discuss progress
- A role for each member of the team which meant they had to communicate with each other eg producing a newsletter, collating monthly figures, managing the holiday rota
- Virtual meetings scheduled at a time convenient to all
- The team should agree how to organise and manage information
- Language training for those who needed it, as meetings were held in English
- Regular checks, in meetings, that everyone was involved and could understand
- Time for the team to set up a team charter and find practical ways to work together

After each virtual meeting Paula reviewed the process with the team to make sure it had been productive for everyone. Clear agendas and action minutes were circulated before and immediately after the meeting.

# START SLOWLY TO ACHIEVE SUCCESS

The secret in working with any team, and especially more complex teams, is to focus on the processes and relationships in the team so that you can build a solid base from which to achieve the task.

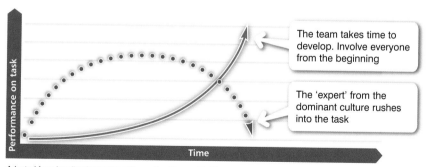

The team takes time to develop. Involve everyone from the beginning

The 'expert' from the dominant culture rushes into the task

*Adapted from Leading International Teams Sue Canney Davidson and Karen Ward, 1999.*

# CREATING HIGH-PERFORMING TEAMS

## REVIEW & ACTIONS

In this section we have looked at:

- Why team work is important
- The stages of team development
- Team effectiveness
- Facilitating a team session
- Building trust in your team
- Working in a complex team
- Developing a communication strategy for virtual working

List three things you have found useful and can use in your job:

1. _____

2. _____

3. _____

# BRINGING IT ALL TOGETHER

# BRINGING IT ALL TOGETHER

## SUMMARY

This Performance Management Pocketbook has provided a range of ideas, tips and techniques to help you to deliver higher performance and engagement with and through your team.

It's worth reviewing your progress on a regular basis:

- Reflect on what ideas are working for you and the team
- What changes are you seeing as a result?
- What new ideas could you put into practice to boost performance and engagement in the organisation?

# THE BENEFITS OF GETTING IT RIGHT

**For you**
- Better overall performance from individuals and teams
- More time to focus on more strategic issues (created through successful use of delegation and coaching)
- Greater satisfaction from seeing people develop and grow

**For your team**
- Clear achievable objectives
- Improved motivation
- Opportunity to develop new skills

**For the organisation**
- Improved bottom line results
- Lower staff turnover
- Improved engagement and staff morale

You now have a toolkit of tips, techniques and approaches to help you make a real difference in the work place.

**Good luck!**

# FURTHER READING

**Engaged, Unleashing your Organizations Potential** Linda Holbeche and Geoffrey Matthews. Jossey-Bass, 2012

**Coaching for Performance** John Whitmore. Nicholas Brealey, 4th edition, 2009

**First Break all the Rules** Marcus Buckingham and Curt Coffman. Pocket Books, 2005

**The Distance Manager** Kimball Fisher and Mareen Duncan Fisher. McGraw Hill, 2001

Other relevant titles from the Management Pocketbooks series:

**Coaching Pocketbook**
Ian Fleming & Allan J.D. Taylor.

**Delegation Pocketbook**
Jon Warner

**Feedback Pocketbook**
Mike Pezet

**Motivation Pocketbook**
Max. A. Eggert

**Tackling Difficult Conversations Pocketbook**
Peter English

**Virtual Teams Pocketbook**
Ian Fleming

**Working Relationships**
Fiona Elsa Dent

## About the Author

**Pam Jones BA MBA**
Pam is a member of Ashridge Business School's open programme management team with responsibility for a suite of programmes encompassing performance management, influencing, leadership and general management skills. She works internationally with a range of organisations to design and deliver development initiatives.

She has also worked for Hongkong Bank and Monash Mount Elisa Business school in Australia and is an accredited executive coach. She has written a number of books *Managing for Performance* (Prentice Hall 2007) *The Impact and Presence Pocketbook* (2004), and *Delivering Exceptional Performance* (Times Pitman, 1996).

**Contact**
Pam can be contacted at: pam.jones@ashridge.org.uk

# Pocketbooks – *available in both paperback and digital formats*

360 Degree Feedback*
Absence Management
Appraisals
Assertiveness
Balance Sheet
Body Language
Business Planning
Career Transition
Coaching
Cognitive Behavioural Coaching
Communicator's
Competencies
Confidence
Creative Manager's
C.R.M.
Cross-cultural Business
Customer Service
Decision-making
Delegation
Developing People
Discipline & Grievance
Diversity*
Emotional Intelligence
Empowerment*
Energy and Well-being
Facilitator's
Feedback
Flexible Working*
Handling Complaints

Handling Resistance
Icebreakers
Impact & Presence
Improving Efficiency
Improving Profitability
Induction*
Influencing
Interviewer's
I.T. Trainer's
Key Account Manager's
Leadership
Learner's
Learning Needs Analysis
Management Models
Manager's
Managing Assessment Centres
Managing Budgets
Managing Cashflow
Managing Change
Managing Customer Service
Managing Difficult Participants
Managing Recruitment
Managing Upwards
Managing Your Appraisal
Marketing
Mediation
Meetings
Memory
Mentoring

Motivation
Negotiator's
Networking
NLP
Nurturing Innovation
Openers & Closers
People Manager's
Performance Management
Personal Success
Positive Mental Attitude
Presentations
Problem Behaviour
Project Management
Psychometric Testing
Resolving Conflict
Reward*
Sales Excellence
Salesperson's*
Self-managed Development
Starting In Management
Storytelling
Strategy
Stress
Succeeding at Interviews
Sustainability
Tackling Difficult Conversations
Talent Management
Teambuilding Activities
Teamworking

Telephone Skills
Thinker's
Time Management
Trainer's
Training Evaluation
Transfer of Learning
Transformative Change
Virtual Teams
Vocal Skills
Webinars
Working Relationships
Workplace Politics
Writing Skills

\* only available as an e-book

## Pocketfiles

Trainer's Blue Pocketfile of
Ready-to-use Activities

Trainer's Green Pocketfile of
Ready-to-use Activities

Trainer's Red Pocketfile of
Ready-to-use Activities

To order please visit us at **www.pocketbook.co.uk**

16.04.15